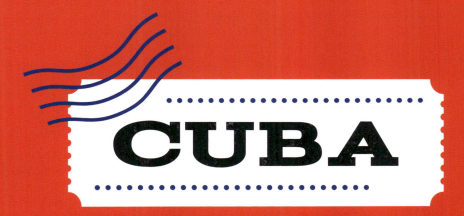

CUBA

R.L. Van

Big Buddy Books
An Imprint of Abdo Publishing
abdobooks.com

abdobooks.com

Published by Abdo Publishing, a division of ABDO, PO Box 398166, Minneapolis, Minnesota 55439. Copyright © 2023 by Abdo Consulting Group, Inc. International copyrights reserved in all countries. No part of this book may be reproduced in any form without written permission from the publisher. Big Buddy Books™ is a trademark and logo of Abdo Publishing.

Printed in the United States of America, North Mankato, Minnesota
102022
012023

THIS BOOK CONTAINS RECYCLED MATERIALS

Design: Emily O'Malley, Mighty Media, Inc.
Production: Mighty Media, Inc.
Editor: Jessica Rusick
Cover Photograph: Kamira/Shutterstock Images
Interior Photographs: Brian Friedman/Shutterstock Images, p. 21; Diy13/iStockphoto, p. 13; duncan1890/iStockphoto, p. 9; edb3_16/iStockphoto, p. 19; flowgraph/iStockphoto, p. 30 (flag); golero/iStockphoto, p. 6 (middle); itsmokko/Shutterstock Images, p. 7 (map); javgutierrez/iStockphoto, p. 26 (left); Javier Galeano/AP Images, p. 11; jfmdesign/iStockphoto, p. 26 (right); Joel Carillet/iStockphoto, p. 28 (bottom right); Kathy Willens/AP Images, p. 27 (top left); lukulo/iStockphoto, pp. 5 (compass), 7 (compass); MaboHH/iStockphoto, p. 25; Manuel Garcia Casado/iStockphoto, p. 27 (top right); Mauro_Repossini/iStockphoto, p. 27 (bottom); Maxim Glass/iStockphoto, p. 15; Nikada/iStockphoto, p. 17; Picasa 2.6/Flickr, p. 28 (top); Pyty/Shutterstock Images, p. 5 (map); Sean Pavone/iStockphoto, p. 6 (top); Sgt. Ryan Hallock/Flickr, p. 29 (bottom); Thomas Faull/iStockphoto, p. 30 (currency); Vadim_Nefedov/iStockphoto, p. 6 (bottom); Wikimedia Commons, pp. 23, 28 (bottom left), 29 (top)
Design Elements: Mighty Media, Inc.
Country population and area figures taken from the CIA World Factbook

Library of Congress Control Number: 2022940512

Publisher's Cataloging-in-Publication Data
Names: Van, R.L., author.
Title: Cuba / by R.L. Van
Description: Minneapolis, Minnesota : Abdo Publishing, 2023 | Series: Countries | Includes online resources and index.
Identifiers: ISBN 9781532199585 (lib. bdg.) | ISBN 9781098274788 (ebook)
Subjects: LCSH: Cuba--Juvenile literature. | Islands of the Caribbean--Juvenile literature. | Cuba--History--Juvenile literature. | Geography--Juvenile literature.
Classification: DDC 917.291--dc23

Passport to Cuba	4
Important Cities	6
Cuba in History	8
An Important Symbol	12
Across the Land	14
Earning a Living	16
Life in Cuba	18
Famous Faces	20
A Great Country	24
Tour Book	26
Timeline	28
Cuba Up Close	30
Glossary	31
Online Resources	31
Index	32

PASSPORT TO CUBA

Cuba is a small island country. It is part of North America. The Caribbean Sea, Atlantic Ocean, and Gulf of Mexico border Cuba. More than 11 million people live there.

IMPORTANT CITIES

Havana is Cuba's **capital** and largest city. It is known for its history, architecture, culture, and entertainment.

Santiago de Cuba is Cuba's second-largest city. It is a center for mining and shipping.

Camagüey is Cuba's third-largest city. It is known for its maze-like design and historic center.

Havana
Population: 2.15 million

Camagüey
Population: 306,152

Santiago de Cuba
Population: 433,099

CUBA

SAY IT

Havana
huh-VA-nuh

Santiago de Cuba
san-tee-AH-goh duh KYOO-buh

Camagüey
kah-mah-GWAY

CUBA IN HISTORY

Cuba's first people were American Indians. In the late 1400s, the Spanish claimed Cuba. Many Native people died under Spanish rule.

In 1898, the United States helped free Cuba from Spain. The United States interfered in Cuba for many more years.

Cuba fought the Ten Years' War to break free from Spanish rule.

Cuba's new government faced problems. Many people died fighting for change.

In the 1950s, three men led a **revolution**. In 1959, Fidel Castro became Cuba's ruler. He limited travel and business between Cuba and other countries. Since then, Castro's party has controlled Cuba. It is now called the **Communist Party of Cuba**.

Fidel Castro died at age 90 in 2016.

AN IMPORTANT SYMBOL

Cuba's flag has blue and white stripes. On the left is a white star inside a red triangle.

Cuba is run by the **Communist** Party of Cuba. The National Assembly of People's Power makes laws. The president is chief of state. The prime minister is head of government.

The white star on Cuba's flag stands for independence.

ACROSS THE LAND

Cuba has a main island and more than 1,600 smaller islands. The country has beaches, farmland, **swamps**, and mountains. It has hundreds of rivers and streams.

Bats, crocodiles, and iguanas live in Cuba. Palm trees, ceiba trees, and many kinds of flowers grow there.

Viñales Valley in Cuba is home to animals and plants found nowhere else in the world.

DID YOU KNOW?

The world's smallest bird, the bee hummingbird, is only found in Cuba.

EARNING A LIVING

• • • • • • • • • • • • •

The government controls most of Cuba's businesses. Some people make tobacco products and beverages. Others have service jobs.

Workers mine nickel, zinc, and copper. Farmers produce sugarcane, rice, fruits, and **cassava**. Fish, shrimp, and lobster come from the ocean.

Cuban tobacco is known worldwide for its quality.

LIFE IN CUBA

Cubans live in cities and **rural** areas. The government is supportive of the arts. Music, dance, and movies are important parts of everyday life.

Popular foods in Cuba include beans, rice, chicken, and pork. Many people drink coffee. Baseball, basketball, boxing, and soccer are favorite sports.

Street performers are part of Cuba's city culture.

DID YOU KNOW?

All schoolchildren in Cuba must wear a uniform.

FAMOUS FACES

Singer Camila Cabello was born in Havana. She moved to Florida at age six. Cabello became famous as a member of the group Fifth Harmony. She went solo in 2016. Her song "Havana" became the number one song in 95 countries.

SAY IT

Camila Cabello
kuh-MEE-luh kuh-BAY-oh

Camila Cabello's full name is Karla Camila Cabello Estrabao.

Athlete Javier Sotomayor was born in Limonar, Cuba. He has won many international high jump titles and two Olympic gold medals. As of 2022, he held world records for indoor and outdoor high jumps.

SAY IT

Javier Sotomayor
*hah-vee-AIR
soh-toh-mye-OHR*

As of 2022, Javier Sotomayor was the only known person to have jumped eight feet (2 m) high.

A GREAT COUNTRY

Cuba is known for its beautiful land and unique culture. The people and places of Cuba help make the world a more interesting place.

For many years, Cuba did not allow new cars to be sent to the islands. So, vintage cars are common there.

If you ever visit Cuba, here are some places to go and things to do!

EAT

Visit a local restaurant for Cuban food, which mixes Spanish, African, and Caribbean styles.

SWIM

Snorkel at Playa Coral, which has pink coral sand, coral reefs, and blue-green waters.

CHEER

Join local baseball fans at a Cuban National Series game.

EXPLORE

Stroll through Old Havana. You can visit museums and play in the neighborhood's historic plazas.

DANCE

Take a class to learn Cuban dances like the mambo, Cuban bolero, or salsa.

1492
Christopher Columbus landed in Cuba. He claimed the land for Spain.

1895
Writer José Julián Martí organized a **revolution** against Spanish rule. He became a Cuban hero.

1959
The Cuban revolution led by Fidel and Raúl Castro and Che Guevara ends. Fidel Castro takes power.

1962
The Soviet Union placed **nuclear weapons** in Cuba. Americans feared it would lead to war. This became known as the Cuban Missile Crisis.

2008

Fidel Castro stepped down. His brother Raúl became president of Cuba.

2019

After 43 years without a prime minister, Cuba amended its constitution to re-create the position.

2012

Hurricane Sandy hit Cuba. It killed eleven people and destroyed thousands of homes.

CUBA
UP CLOSE

Official Name
Republic of Cuba

Flag

Population
11,008,112 (2022 est.)
84th-most-populated country

Total Area
42,803 square miles
(110,860 sq km)
105th-largest country

Official Language
Spanish

Capital
Havana

Currency
Cuban peso

Form of Government
Communist state

National Anthem
"La Bayamesa"
("The Bayamo Song")

GLOSSARY

capital—a city where government leaders meet.

cassava—a starchy root vegetable. It is also called yuca.

Communist (KAHM-yuh-nihst)—relating to a form of government in which ways of creating wealth, such as land, factories, and machines, are owned by the state. They are shared among the people as needed.

nuclear weapon—a bomb or missile that uses nuclear energy, which leads to very powerful and dangerous explosions.

revolution—the forced overthrow of a government for a new system.

rural—of or relating to open land away from towns and cities.

swamp—land that is wet and often covered with water.

ONLINE RESOURCES

To learn more about Cuba, please visit **abdobooklinks.com** or scan this QR code. These links are routinely monitored and updated to provide the most current information available.

INDEX

animals, 14, 15, 16
Atlantic Ocean, 4, 5

businesses, 10, 16

Cabello, Camila, 20, 21
Camagüey, 6, 7
Caribbean Sea, 4, 26
Castro, Fidel, 10, 11, 28, 29
Castro, Raúl, 28, 29
Columbus, Christopher, 28
Communist Party of Cuba, 10, 12

dancing, 18, 27

flag, 12, 13, 30
food, 16, 18, 26

government, 10, 12, 18, 28, 29, 30
Guevara, Che, 28
Gulf of Mexico, 4, 5

Havana, 6, 7, 20, 27, 30

language, 30

Martí, José Julián, 28

natural resources, 16, 17
North America, 4

plants, 14, 15, 16, 17
Playa Coral, 26
population, 4, 7, 30

Santiago de Cuba, 6, 7
size, 4, 30
Sotomayor, Javier, 22, 23
Soviet Union, 28
Spain, 8, 9, 26, 28
sports, 18, 22, 23, 27

United States, 5, 8